To Dawn —
May you find all
the joys that give
you wings —
Gary

MARROW, MUSCLE, FLIGHT

POEMS

Gary Boelhower

Wildwood River Press
Duluth, Minnesota

Wildwood River Press
1748 Wildwood Road
Duluth, MN 55804

www.wildwoodriver.com

ISBN: 978-0-9843777-4-9

Library of Congress Control Number: 2011935068

ACKNOWLEDGMENTS

"Blackbirds" was published in *Freshwater Review*, 2011.

"Distance" was published (as "From A Distance") in *Beloved on the Earth: 150 Poems of Grief and Gratitude*. Holy Cow! Press, 2009.

"A Day Like Today," "And You Say," "Lake Superior" and "Sanctuary" were published in *Trail Guide to the Northland Experience in Prints and Poetry*. Calyx Press Duluth, 2005.

"Hawk Ridge" was published in *County Lines: 87 Minnesota Counties 130 Minnesota Poets*. Loonfeather Press, 2008.

This book is made possible through a fiscal year 2011 Career Development grant from the Arrowhead Regional Arts Council (www.aracouncil.org) which is funded in part with money from the Minnesota Arts and Cultural Heritage Fund as appropriated by the Minnesota State Legislature with money from the vote of the people of Minnesota on November 4, 2008; an appropriation from the Minnesota State Legislature; The McKnight Foundation.

Cover design by Cecilia Lieder (www.cecilialieder.com)
Cover Art © Cecilia Lieder, Heart of a Peony: Red
Cover Photo © Amanda Hansmeyer (www.shutterstoriesonline.com)

GRATITUDE

To Sheila Packa, Pamela Mittlefehldt, Kyle Elden, Cal Benson, Bernadette Savage, Dennis Herschbach and Greg Opstad for weekly challenges and helpful suggestions at poetry group. To Pamela Mittlefehldt for close reading of the entire manuscript twice, critical reflection, and sharp insight. To Deborah Cooper for encouragement incarnate. To Sam Black for providing opportunities for reading and believing in possibilities. To Cecilia Lieder for the love of poetry, the inspiration of art, and high tea. To Sheila Packa and Kathy McTavish for artistic passion and believing in fine books of poetry.

To the memory of Robert C. Archer whose love and passion for beauty and truth have blessed my life in ways uncountable.

To Gary B. Anderson for love, marriage, and all that grows in the gardens of our delight.

CONTENTS

I.

II.

III.

I.

WHEN DID YOU KNOW

Where the wing grows from the body,
in that intersection that shapes itself
to air and lift, blue cells whispering flight,
where you touched me and filled
my questions with buoyant light.

So many days in my clumsy body,
damping its persistent fires, deaf to the words
it loves, the music without a name, starving
the proud flesh and all its wild hungers.

When they ask me that queer question
"When did you know you were gay?"
I will say the helix and the blood, marrow,
muscle and every vital cell and when you
touched me where the wing grows
from the body with your wet soft lips.

DANCES AT THE WEDDING

I.
I drift in memory with my daughter, the bride,
swirl of white lace, whisper of satin and my
feeble words spoken over her shoulder
about the awkward eternity of a father's love,
letting go and remembering everything.

All the images crowd into these moments
on the dance floor while everyone watches:
first wild tantrum of the twos, screaming
and kicking her objection to the necessity
of snowsuits or rules of any kind, her
stubborn persistence, her absolute faith.

The theatrical announcement at the preschool
Christmas play: "Let the wild rumpus begin."
How she is poised like an accomplished
actress, full presence and commanding voice.

Her questions about everything, the sweet
desire to know the caterpillar and the chrysalis,
the monarch in the jar that must be let go
moments after seeing it, to fly on yellow morning air.

Step, step, turn, tears on the white lace,
memories like a torrent rushing between
the banks of this song, finally my arms
wrap around her whole precious life.

II.
Divorced but still dancing, the mother
of the bride and I, the touch of other tangos
in our hearts and my grateful words spoken
over her shoulder, how amazing it all is,
from the storm of passion to the scramble
of making a nest for another fragile breath.

All the images crowd into these moments
on the dance floor while everyone watches:
moonlight kisses and remodeling every room,
diapers, sawdust, the mortgage and the small
arguments, the pictures for each grade, art projects
for the Christmas tree year after happy year.

And the distance, the slow rotting that we
didn't know until the foundation shifted,
the crumbling of dreams that wracks the gut,
the awful grief that brings us back alive.

Step, step, turn, pulling her closer to say
how dear the memories, the good and the hard,
how the dance is what gets us here, carried
by our own crazy river of darkness and light.

III.
My new lover and I dance in the far
parking lot under the ravenous stars,
my words whispered over his shoulder.
Take the hand of this secret love.
All the images crowd into these moments
in the parking lot while no one is watching:
stories that connect at the gay fathers group,
brassy questions and copious flowers,
how tenderly the body learns to trust
the deep currents of the river, the pull of light.
Step, step, turn, drawing him closer to say
let us dance until this darkness turns to dawn.

TELLING THE STORY

Steel words bolted and double bolted
arched and reaching from my new truth
to your young mind. I worry over

every weld, every cable, every turn
of the wrench of logic. This bridge
must bear the freight of failures

and the tonnage of a father's love.
Years in the making, telling the story
over and over to the journal,

to the mirror, to the friend who
keeps saying the bridge will hold.
I want you to know that all the planets

still spin in their places, that nothing is
different though everything is changed.
I want you to know. These are the hands

that balanced your wobbling bicycle, held
the nail when you needed both arms to lift
the hammer, steadied your leg while the doctor

stitched the bleeding gash, cradled your body
and rocked your raging fever to sleep.
These are the hands that will always be home.

Finally, we sit at the kitchen table
with plates of pot roast and mashed potatoes.
"I have to tell you something." The story

pours out, emptiness of divorce, the lonely
apartment, seeing them on Wednesdays
and every other weekend, like drowning

in loss, my lungs pounding and burning.
As I start across, the bridge is a tightrope
straining with each syllable, each sweaty silence.

It has been a long swim in a second womb but I
know now that I am a gay man, that I can accept
my own flesh and its perfect feelings. I hope

you will still love me. I am the same father
who cherished you since before you were born.
The bolts didn't rattle loose, the cables didn't snap.

There were no questions, no gasps, no turning
away, only "Yeah, OK." "Not a big deal." The steel
wasn't steel at all, no perfect logic, only filaments

of love woven between a father and two sons,
those threads of everyday infinite affection.

TO LOVE AGAIN

What would it be like to love again?
To walk out on that thin filament
and trust my balance? With each step
I move farther from safety, into the middle,
where suspended I feel most alive,
like I am performing my life
not for the crowd but for the taut wire itself,
following the way it stretches out before me.
How it beckons me into the light,
the open air, where the only thing
I have to forget is the net that isn't there.

RESTAURANT RESERVATIONS

Facing you safely
with a square of pressed white distance
and the usual condiments between us,
I swirl my Merlot. But
do you notice the small tremble
in the voice, the knees shaking
under the table, how I throw
against all hope a shiny penny
into the fountain
of your curiosity and hunger,
wishing for not too much?
Can you feel the race
of blood and desire,
the deep currents of doubt
where no light reaches?

THIS HOLY LONGING

I could stay forever, the way your arm
is wrapped around my chest and your quiet
breath keeps whispering into my neck,
a soft litany of comfort and belonging.
When you finally awake, our submission
to each other's wishes again, the songs
that a body knows by heart. I ask you
to stand next to the open window
so I can see the flowing river of your
body shine in the morning light.

On the early breeze the long lonely whistle
of a train, the temptation of wanderlust,
the stubborn thought that tomorrow
you will rather be with someone else.

Somewhere a robin begins the green
song of spring and I reach for your hand
and pull you down to the bed still warm
with our passion and our hope. I offer
a silent prayer in the temple of your body
as my lips anoint your holy longing.

STAGE SET

The midnight director meets with me under the glaring lamps
in front of the stage set. Black paint is still drying, sending
out its sweet nausea. He says I can choose what my life
looks like, he can design and build anything. Even
mountains of adventure and passion, streams of clear thought,
a log cabin in sunshine next to the wild river and reaching pines.
Anything is possible, wood, steel, paint, imagination,
and his crew of experts, muscled, clear-eyed, eager to begin.

They are watching us, waiting for directions, their fingers
nervously resting on their belts full of tools, one keeps
pulling and releasing a yellow yard from his tape measure.
The director turns away from them, pulls me close,
and whispers, "But you will have to brace the foundation.
They will take care of everything on stage, but you
will have to crawl underneath and run beams from one
post to another, four by fours of faith from one sagging
doubt to the next stark question. And then on each beam,
you must place a prayer, written on white paper with black
ink and folded four times and nailed in place. This is the hard
work," he says, "down below, with the single hot bulb at the end
of the long orange extension cord, with hammer, nails, saw,
on your back in the dirt, in the small spaces, with the cobwebs
in your face, sweating over each syllable of prayer."

ONE MORE GENERATION

One more generation pushes like the sun
through the morning mist and I can only
stand and pant with you and wait and pray
my useless prayers that the ancient
rhythms will work their wisdom again
as they always have and always will.

I can only stand and watch
you breathe and rub the round planet
of your belly that ripples with
waves that rhyme with ocean and orbit.
Teach me a new language to sing
the rhythms of the moon that ebb
and flow in you with the warm
iron hands of labor and destiny.

The child dances in the only
ocean that matters, dives down
down in the soft darkness,
and the urge that comes from magma
and seed and gravity collects in your
animal breathing and you do what
must be done like rivers and seasons.

Such mysteries will not be parsed
by hormones, muscles, tissues.
These names are too small
for the salty wisdom that cradles
his folded body, for his bright
bright lungs that wail the light awake.

NAME

My daughter says "opa" and hands
me Luigi with his ten perfect fingers and toes.
My arm curls into cradle
a safe shelter for the universe.
I whisper his name
into the soft whirl of his pink ear.

Luigi wonder of the silver river
Luigi touch of dawn drenched sky
Luigi song of endless surprise
Luigi sweet comfort
Luigi bright word.

I will call you galaxy
every cell a star
all the light
years of hope settling in the silky
creases of your flesh.

FIRST DEPLOYMENT

My Marine son came home for Christmas
wrapped his strong arms around me
pulled me to his steel chest and kissed me
as he did when he was a child before
his cheek felt the smooth stock of the rifle
and his hands learned how to pull the pin
and hold the lever and throw a grenade
at a machine gun position and we drank
wine and he told the story all over again
about his first deployment crossing the border
into Iraq on his nineteenth birthday in a seven
ton truck headed for Ramadi where they hoped
to learn the names of the citizens and help them
rebuild their schools and hospitals and how
it didn't turn out that way how his platoon
took the officials to inspect the newly repaired
school how they were giving out soccer balls
when the rocket propelled grenade struck
the group of thirty small children and scattered
their bodies and parts of their bodies around
the school yard how the blood ran on the sidewalk
and soaked into the dirt how the docs worked
frantically on the wounded children how they
didn't stop to put on their latex gloves how they
emptied their first aid kits and started using
bandanas and t-shirts to bandage the wounds
how he and his fellow Marines set up defenses
around the school yard so the docs could keep
working as they all waited for the ambulances
and then the second RPG that took off the legs
of Bolding at the knees how my son tied
the tourniquets while the blood spurted while
Bolding kept yelling that his legs felt tangled
someone please untangle them and we drank
to Bolding who died a few days later the first
casualty of war in my son's platoon and then
we went to the water park and plunged down
the coiling slides and laughed and watched

14

the little children splash and shout and scream
with glee and he told me it is very important
to keep your skills sharp so he often goes
to the firing range on weekends to practice.

ASKING THE QUESTION

Neither the father nor the son asks
the question that burns behind their eyes.

What do you do after you fight in a war,
pull the trigger, see the blood run, feel
bits of shrapnel bite into your face a fraction
from your eyes, tighten a tourniquet around
your dying friend's stumps of legs?

They work and sweat side by side, building
the wall of a new flower bed. Both know
the language of war cannot be translated.
The father searches in vain for words to speak
his hope, like rock and earth, lift and settle.
Their only attempt to call upon the future is to
remember the past, the cord wrapped around
the son's neck and his blue body silent while
one nurse suctioned his mouth and another
slapped the bottoms of his feet for those
eternal moments while the father prayed, and then
the surge of life and his first wailing, warrior cry.

The son and the father are silent, the noon blaze is hot
on their backs and out of the east a breeze, a still small voice.

EYES WIDE OPEN EXHIBIT

I walk the rows of boots, from Montana to Florida,
from New York to California, no state spared
this particular grief that war brings. The names
are familiar: Todd, Tommy, Linda, Jose;
three Brians from Illinois. In every row there are
too many 19s and 21s, like finding a field of flowers
about to open mangled and sheared by some cold machine.
And then 36, father of three, the youngest still
dreams his Dad's face on any night with noises.
23, engaged, planning the marriage in letters, and now
the vows are curses. 51, soon to be a grandfather
never to count or kiss those tiny toes and fingers.
I imagine their faces and the hearts of those who love
them breaking open, and the photographs they
displayed at the funerals, the proud 5-year old
in his soccer uniform, her high school graduation picture
with the band, the fisherman holding his gaping muskie
on that impossibly bright afternoon, each one
a precious story, a whole language lost to war.

I move then to another language, the circle of shoes
that are everyone's shoes. The names here are not
familiar; but the faces are the same, the dreams, the grinding
grief. Here the numbers are 8 months, 2 years, 10, 66.
And then out of the circle of shoes I hear a mother's story.
I see her. She pauses, swallows hard the bitterness,
a taste of metal lodged deep in her throat.
She bites her lip, pulls the black veil closer around her face,
shifts the tender weight of her 3-month old son
on her hip; then she continues her story with eyes wide
open, dry as the desert. She says there are uncles
who will teach him that his father was a martyr,
a holy man of courage, but she will tell him
how he could coax stars out of the sky with his songs.

AFTER THE NEWS

Out walking the dogs
to get away from the news,
I followed a father and his two daughters
on their way home from the bus stop.
Eight and five I would guess.
The eight year old was all business,
deep in conversation with her dad,
something about seeds and what's inside.
The five year old was straggling behind.
Every ten steps she would discover
something amazing, a leaf to touch,
a pine cone to explore, a different leaf,
the heaved up sidewalk so she had to
put her foot on it like a teeter totter.
Even though her father promised snacks,
it didn't matter, the world was too
full to rush over. Her thin body
would bend in half, her eyes just inches
from a worm on the edge of the sidewalk.

All the while, every time she stopped
to touch something, I was thinking
of cluster bombs as small as her fist
that mothers and fathers make in factories
and pray the seeds will never be planted.

Years from now in Lebanon
they will still be warning the children
not to touch, but the children
with their soft and curious hands
will be children.

ASK THE CHILDREN

Ask the children about the world
the barefoot children with their eyes
wide open cameras collecting
every bit of light and pain.

Ask the children about the world
the ones hiding underneath the
slain bodies of their mothers
and their sisters and their brothers.

Ask the children how the warm
blood of their families matted
their hair and seeped like a keening
shriek into the whorl of their ears.

In Rwanda they asked three
thousand children and four
hundred eighty said they hid
under the bodies of the dead.

They felt that weight.
One talked of his sister's face
staring staring but he
did not dare whisper goodbye.

If you do not believe the children
ask the mothers who hear
the screams of their daughters
night after night in the dark

their arms aching with emptiness
their breasts swollen with unsucked
mercy their throats still rasping
still calling the names of their hope.

How will we ask the children
and the mothers about the world?
On our knees? weeping? and what
shall we do with our hands?

HEAVEN

that in each body, however obscured or recast,
is the divine body—common, habitable—

song of wave or mouth
froth of water licking sand

tendril tearing through packed earth
wisps of white racing in yellow wind

everything that can't be contained
holy wells in the generous geography
of your body

sirens singing in my cells
heaven isn't any place without flesh

your hungry and merciful mouth
and the play of light
on the breeze kissed

bed after a night of giving and taking
collisions of continents tectonic shifts
dance dream redeemed

EXPERIMENT

Disheveled sheets of clouds fly
before the face of a September
half moon as we walk along
the lake hand in hand listen to its
soft murmur and fall in love
again as if for the first time still
wondering if it can last if you
want me if the silence between us
is promise or betrayal and you
pull me to a park bench
you lean into me and our lips
meet and I watch you close your eyes
before I close mine and pull you
closer and wonder if every kiss
is a song a bell a seed
war or peace taking or giving
some pure sign of hope
experiment in breath death silence.

THE RULES

Plan everything, go over it in your mind
a hundred times and then just let it happen.

Bring dozens of white daisies, their faces still
warm from the sun, still jostling each other like tea dancers
their voices careening into the sky.

Pour the extravagant champagne recklessly
so we have to lick the foam off the top of the glasses.

Lead me to the bedroom with just our little fingers
entwined and stop in the hallway and press my back
against the rough wall with your growing passion.

Light two candles. Open the window to the warm breeze.

Take your shirt off first so I can begin to map
the journey I will navigate through your wilderness.

Sprawl on the white sheet with every cell open
with every molecule longing.

Don't worry about timing. Lose control.

Give me all your attention.

Keep your eyes open.

Forget about death.

ALL DAY IN BIRCHES

Have you watched the sun dawn
on birches, how the rays sneak
into a dark forest and the birches
light up, going from gray to parchment
to dazzle and their green vowels
rise and fall on the morning
breeze like a sacred chant in a lustrous
basilica domed in robin egg blue?

Have you noticed how the birches
unwrap themselves on the hot
afternoons of summer, how the soft
hands of light play up and down
their spines until the birches
open another layer and the sun enters?

Their swaying bodies and the tender
light embrace all day long, whisper
to each other, sigh into the evening's
lengthening shadows. Even the leaving
is lovely, the sun blushes its farewell.

What would it be like if you loved
your body like this, just as you are,
if you loved your life like this?
From dawn to dusk, if you let the sun enter?

A DAY LIKE TODAY

On a day
like today
when the clear syllables
of spring rain sing on the warm
shingles, sudden thunder quickens our hearts,
distant bells ring a muffled hymn
through the lazy hours,
musty green
moss

on the trunks
of the swaying
cedars shines like the thumb
prints of a God who roams the garden,
whistling, with a hoe propped on his weary shoulder
and promises spilling from his pockets,
when you turn toward me
with your Sunday
smile, your lips

relentless,
your skin tasting
like the everlasting earth,
I can believe the tiny seeds planted
under yesterday's sun soften in their straight rows,
their risky green wishes swelling
toward speech -- flower, fruit, seed,
the whole perfect
story.

NOTICE

I am done now with those years
when everything still matters
and the measurements are made
by someone else's yardstick,
when how do I look and am I
enough echo in the mirror.
Mostly now it is the internal scale
that I wrestle with, the big
question about doing what I am
called to do in the way that I
can best do it. The question
now is about silence and the journey,
sitting still and the changes that must come.
What streets should I be marching in?
On what bright afternoons should I be singing
in the forest of birches? Mostly now,
the call is to notice
the kind faces of the daisies,
shine and strut of the arguing crows,
the hunger and the silent
rivers of violence and blood.

RUINS

The awe of mountains is their weather-beaten sides, standing
through the storms of centuries, blasted with sand, pummeled
with ice, their gorges deepen, their saddles wear smooth.

The marvel of rivers is their wild wayward rumble,
banks cut deep, the bouldered underbelly of rapids
or the silted shallows of the mellow meander.

The beauty of trees is their gnarled persistence, eating
the rusted wire of the fence line, bearing in their bodies
the long conversation with light, gravity, wind.

And so the body goes, the slow slide into the sea. Creases
of laughter and worry deepen. Fingers stiffen and twist.
The belly sags, the abs go slack. A simple burden lodges
for days in the muscles of the back. The entropy of flesh,
rusting gears, glow of wisdom, old flannel comfort.

Disheveled sacrament of senses, praise for all the moments:
garden dirt sifted through fingers with green spring dreams,
the rush of dawn like a first kiss revisited over and over,
sweet sunset casting its purple spell over the sighing lake.
The hands you've held through the final breath, opening
somehow.
The tiny toes you've counted and nibbled into giggles.
The first words, the last words, the tender moans of sex,
the scent of lilacs, lilies, and the rich chocolate earth.

Yes, you are ruined into softness, memories and memories
filling the small sanctuaries of every pulsing cell.

SPLINTERS OF LIGHTNING

He didn't speak English but he could do anything
it seemed to me, especially in his tar-papered
tool shed with its dirt floor so you were always
standing on the earth. White thick hair just long enough

to stand straight and stiff, square jaw, eyebrows
like tumbling whitecaps. He chased the children
out of his plum tree with a hatchet, shouting
at them in Dutch, the sharp blade gleaming.

Every blade was sharp—knife, axe, sickle,
spade tip even; every blade honed to the perfect
edge on his grinding stone. Nothing was more
wondrous to me than the way he sharpened things.

The perfect rhythm of the shuttle, the whir
of the round stone, and the sound of the two
hard worlds, one grinding the other to a useful edge.
The sparks flying off like splinters of lightning.

Every few weeks the blades would have to be set
right again, a slow wearing away of their bodies
so they could do their work. I can remember only
one day when he wouldn't let me in, when I

stood in the cold outside the shed listening
to the wheel turn, the terrible clash of hard worlds.
It was in early January and the day before
we had taken our skates off their hooks in the attic

where they waited to cut a perfect arc in the ice.
Why not let me in to see the playful skates
sharpened to their most graceful edge?
He wouldn't answer but mother told me.

After he came to the new world he had a daughter,
his youngest child, born like a promise in America.
On Christmas day, he gave her fine leather skates

with shining blades like the ones he wore on the canals
in the old country. She never put her feet in them,
she died on a cold, cold day in early January.

PRAYER AT ONE HUNDRED

When he was one hundred someone asked him to say
a prayer he knew by heart, had said for decades
through the long voyage, the homes he built,
the tragedy of a young daughter's death,
radio and cars, TV and flight,
the moon walk he watched fingering his beads.

The Dutch words rumbled out of him,
his eyes closed, one guttural grinding into another,
picking up speed, the words pulled faster and faster
by the locomotive of his well oiled mind;
his face flushed and the deep breaths after.

This was the way he did things. Every night
the rosary like a stampede of human needs.
Before we ended our part of the prayer, he launched
into the next Hail Mary like another chore that must be done.

He refused to learn English or buy an oil furnace.
At eighty-five he still chopped wood and tended his acre
of garden, every row straight and not a single weed.

He would hold a baby on his lap long enough
for the picture to be snapped, the only time I saw him smile.

I don't know if he was happy, a question never asked.

But there was work and pain and bread.

MENDING

Grandma came to live with us after grandpa died.
She was almost incorporeal, slight, stooped, quiet.

Ground down by the hard soil of two failed farms
and one that made it, long decades of not giving up.

Whisper of a body, wisps of gray hair framing
her sunken cheeks but her hands were always

moving. Peel, slice, stir, but mostly stitch.
She called it mending and sat for hours weaving

a web of repair over the holes in socks. The places
grown thin and weak, like the elbows of shirts,

she patched. The frayed collars and cuffs, every
place that rubbed or chafed against the world,

she would make like new again with her close,
even stitches. It was a kind of music, the slight

percussion of the thimble, the song of thread
unspooling, the rhythm of entrance, exit, glide.

But more than music, bent under her small circle of light,
she made things whole again, she set the world right.

SEEDS

The little seeds, some as small as eyelashes,
others shining half moons, some black
and armored, wait in their glossy packets
with their grown-up pictures on the front
and on the back all the directions you need,
sun or shade, how many days to wait until
their green gusto shouts through the soil
and, most importantly, how deep, thumbnail
or first joint on the index finger—that's how
she taught us. She believed in the earth
and the rhythms of the world, peas planted
on the dark side of the moon when the nights
still chattered with frost, lettuces with a dusting
of the finest soil and always over everything
a prayer, kneeling in the dirt at the edge
of the garden, not a trace of life amid the dry
sticks on which hung the pictures and their beautiful
names: Straight Eight cucumbers, Black Beauty
zucchini, Cherry Belle radishes, Paris Island romaine,
as if by planting them you could enter another
country or even a better version of yourself,
arranging the future in rows evenly spaced
and the right distance apart. The best and most
difficult lesson was gratitude for whatever came up,
for however much sun the summer brought.
"You do your part," she said, "throw the potato peels
and the coffee grounds on the compost pile, follow
the directions, and everything you get is a blessing."
There was always more than enough, brown bags
brimming for neighbors up and down the street.
And when it rained, she taught us to dance in it.

OUT OF NOTHING

Standing in front of the long blackboard
filled with an equation that read like the Greek
alphabet with a voice like delicate china plates
breaking, the professor said, "...continual
fluctuations in the nothingness are generating
and subsuming innumerable universes."

Long before string theory, my father
lived in two different worlds. When
he was on the up side of drunk,
he used to slap his big belly like a drum
as he sat on the couch in the dark
usually around midnight. The only light
was the glowing tip of his cigarette, the only sound
the thump of his belly and his Mill's brothers songs.
At some point he would hit the down side
of drunk, a different world with no music.

I don't think my mother liked equations, at least
she didn't keep track of absences or betrayals.
Every morning she would open the curtains
and stand breathing and smiling, her face
lifted toward the sun, even on the rainy days,
even after those nights when all the music stopped.

Seemingly out of nothing the innumerable universes.
Every Saturday morning she would fill a huge
tin pan with flour, water, salt, yeast and knead
the white dough with her gnarled fingers.
She would let it rise and punch it down
and let it rise again. Then she would kneel
on the floor in front of the oven and bless
the mounded loaves as she slid them into the heat.

LOON CALL

If you hear it once
it will remember you
and forever all your hungers.
You will long for it to lift out of the mist,
to break open the dawn like the first green fingers of spring.

You will want
to be surprised by it,
jolted awake, visited by angels,
lost in utter aloneness, called by name to drop
down into the guts of the world, to feel its molten fire.

Is it laughter
or desperate supplication?
Can you ever tell the two apart?
When in his drunken rage he kicked my mother
what came out of her mouth was a cry like this.

CHINA CUPS

These china tea cups were her only luxury, gilded
rims, scrolling handles, perfect painted flowers

and the porcelain so fine and delicate.
Everything her life was not allowed.

She insisted that we use them on bright
Sunday afternoons. Half the fun was choosing—

the pedestal footed mother of pearl that gleamed
with elegant roses, the opalescent vessel

with nuts and grapes perfectly painted,
the fluted octagon like the blossom of a giant tulip.

With the white tablecloth and the spritz cookies
and these tea cups, we were in a different world.

The sunken pink couch, the stacks of old magazines,
the stained yellow linoleum almost disappeared.

But, as children do, we bumped and dropped
and broke them, never on purpose.

She would collect the tiny shards
and fit them back together like a surgeon.

Only in the harshest light, could you see
the small fissures, the almost invisible

lines where everything came apart.

BLACK VELVET

My father always stopped at the bar
after work and he usually didn't come home
until supper was almost over,
even when Mom fixed one of his favorites
and she would call Connie's Corner Tavern
and plead with him. It always

pissed him off when she called.
He would saunter in later than ever
and she would warm up his plate of food
and set it in front of him without a word.
But one day he came home early
with a three legged big mutt

trailing behind him, a ragged scrap
of black velvet draped over a cage of bones.
There were places where his coat shined
and you could see the dog he could have been.
I gave him a huge bowl of table scraps
soaked in milk and he wolfed it down

while I knelt next to his brown eyes,
even though my father said, "Don't
get too close, we don't know this dog."
I made a bed for him outside in the corner
of the porch out of the wind, four old blankets
when one would have been enough. He left

after three days, three days that I ran home
at noon and again after school to sit next to his
weary whistle of breath and stroke his dark coat.
I think I could have loved him if he would have stayed.

WATCHING DEATH COME

Mostly the waiting and what happens before your eyes.
The small failures of her frail machinery, an arm
that won't work anymore, so she asks to be washed.
By now I am beyond embarrassment and the polite
fences of modesty. Necessity and devotion, a ministration
to the body that is slowly turning to shadow.

Someone says you usually die like you've lived.
She never says a negative word. Even now,
when all she relies on turns against her, legs, lungs, heart,
she does not complain. She apologizes for them
and retreats inside to some bright silence
from which her stories and smiles shine out.

Today the distance between bed and bathroom
is a great journey that takes all her strength.
She is an Everest climber gasping at thin air.
For the ten shuffling steps back to bed, I do
the cautious dance of a human crutch and feel
her china bones under the loose skin. The hard
part is the little pirouette at the end, close
to the edge; then letting her down easy
so she doesn't break. With a deep sigh, she asks
for blankets and I tuck them in around
the shrinking outline of her body, bring them
up under her chin, kiss her sagging cheek,
push back the curtains so she can watch the circus
of jubilant leaves like trapeze artists soaring
through the big top tent of autumn afternoon. I notice
on each leaf stem the little swelling where it attaches
to the branch. I wonder how that strong bond that survives
the storm winds of summer loosens in the night,
softens its hold as the sun retreats, how it knows when.

MOTHER'S DAISIES

I am simply watering the flowers
when the glinting edge of this golden
daisy cuts like a scalpel and lays open
my memory and the raw
grief of that final goodbye.
Here in the garden on an ordinary
Saturday afternoon and I am walking
behind your casket heaped
with bunches of your flowers
picked wild and glowing
from your disheveled garden.
It was your last obvious gift,
a banquet of colors and shapes,
dance of sheer delight in earthy
sacred things. There is an ache
that comes when the colors of blossoms
click a primordial code, never expected.
So I stand in the garden, between
the rows of beans and the drifts
of cosmos, your favorite place,
remembering the flowers you gave away,
blossom by blossom, still blooming.

KEPT SECRETS

Sitting at the top of the wooden ladder
to the unfinished upstairs I listened
to the shouts and curses, then the slap
which meant I had to do something
with my small shaking body to make him stop.

But she still wept when he died, more
than I could understand. She poured the bottles
from his last case of beer one by one down the drain
so the whole house smelled as if he had just
walked in the door late again from the tavern.

We brought his body home to his small kingdom
where the children learned to keep secrets and not
ask questions, to make up excuses why their friends
couldn't come over and why he wouldn't
be at the parent-teacher conference or the ballgame.

On the long night of vigil, kneeling next to his body
and his silent hands and the silent roses, I saw him
sitting in the shade of the purple lilacs, next to his wildly
growing garden. I heard the baseball game playing
on his radio and him cheering, cheering for the underdog.

SHAVING BRUSH

Always after death, the dividing,
favorite fictions posed as memories,
shirts still in their boxes and books unread

hoping yet for some kind of connection.
The only thing I asked for was
his shaving brush, not because

it was beautiful or expensive
or made from some exotic wood.
Plastic worn smooth by his daily

hand, the bristles bore the shape
of his face. In that brush, I could
smell him, hear his grumbling ritual

every morning as the razor cut through
the stubble of eight or ten bottles
of beer drunk the night before and three

packs of cigarettes that graveled in his throat.
Day in day out the walk to the paper mill,
the small insults from his father,

the not enough paycheck, the overdue
bills, the bags of hand-me-downs
from the neighbors left at the door.

Still, every day, the brush would ring
like music against the ceramic soap mug
and the sun would rise, he almost never

yelled or threw things in the morning.
He was more himself, some days
even a small song as he lathered his face

with the sweet soap and wiped it
from his soft lips. And sometimes
on Saturdays, I would stand on a stool

next to the sink and he would touch
my cheeks with those tender
bristles and paint a smile on my face.

DISTANCE

The slight shudder as the plane lifts,
surrenders its earthly obligations.
Details blur into patterns of patchwork.
Highways and rivers, cursive loops
and lines on the diary of acres, miles, lifetimes.
From this distance I can forgive you
again. Boy Scout award dinners without you,
the only words of love slurred after a litany
of beers softens your raw edges, the fear
of another fight with mom, threatening
fists, curses, thrown things. This grief
has been a slow letting go of the small
failures of your fatherhood. From this high
window, I have a larger view, your own
father's insults and judgments, the low
wages, unpaid bills, power turned off,
your dead sister never mentioned.
Not excuses, just a way of seeing.
This grief is a long loneliness of not
feeling the touch you so wanted to give.

IN MY RED CHECKERED GINGHAM SHORTS

The long hot slide with its big bumps
and the gravel at the bottom.
All the cousins at the family picnic
laughing as I climb down the stairs
backward, no tears, no air.

Here I am again
as the masseur digs into my back muscles.

... if I swallowed hard and launched myself
... if I never thought I could and never tried
... if I stayed behind again and played with the toddlers
        in the shade
... if dad walked over and took my hand or lifted me
        onto his shoulders

The masseur pulls my arms hard behind me and says,
"To open your heart to the world."
He counsels me to stand straight and tall and breathe
as if this were the most natural thing in the world.

He doesn't notice when I lift the young boy
in the red checkered gingham shorts onto my shoulders.

FATHER

Forgiveness is not an act
of pride or weakness
but a way of meeting him
in a small clearing
you create with memory,
sunlight, silence;
look into the mirror
of his face.

Forgiveness doesn't run away.
It can't forget
but remembers all
the music, not only
the lamentations.

Walk into the house now
without being afraid, without
those heavy shoulders,
without listening so intently
to the voices, listening
for anger or the dark silence
that meant you had to be careful.

Unclench those small hands,
say your name into the mirror
and let the whole story echo
in your bones, the laughter
and the curses, the wounds
and the simple gifts.

MEMORY OF MYSELF

who I think I am isn't anything real but a heap
of found objects piled and scattered year after year
curious how some things stick some seeds catch
so the smell of warm yeast kneaded into dough
can do a number on my heart time travel me
to that small kitchen flour dust and humming heat
how she would fold and stretch the dough work
it over and over as she told about the rattle
snakes in the wood pile in Montana and how her dad
broke horses in a way that was kind made them gentle
and easy to ride but the land was stubborn and dry
so they moved to Minnesota where another farm
went belly up but not without seasons of laughter
and hunger but always the bread that her mother made
every Saturday every season and cinnamon rolls
usually with lard but sometimes butter sweet as sweet
corn how the sun would shine hot at the swimming hole
always after the threshing after she got all the crickets
out of her pockets how all those grains of wheat
were thrashed ground sifted kneaded so that I can't
separate any thing from any thing else or if I did
it would just be telling a story as if it had a beginning
or an end as if life could be imagined without bread
as if I could be myself without the yeast of her voice

SANCTUARY

Right here in this small
bright clearing among
the reaching emerald branches,
I plant my heart like the seed
of everything possible, everything
to hope for, to believe in.

Right here where the sweet
sweat of earth rises from this mulch
of moss and decaying needles,
from this mix of shit and stardust,
and mingles with the stinging scent
of pine. The tall trunks sway
like the hot hips of God in their
birthing dance and the vital
vernix of spring seeps from
every pore in the warming bark.

This is the Eden of desire, the genesis
garden where a heart can break
open like a promise, where a body
can stretch its endless longings
and trust the river of its own blood.

This is the original story, before
the tree of knowledge, before we made
the jealous gods in the image of our
fears, before the curse of shame.
This is the garden of grace, the long
sigh of belonging, breath of home.

II.

AND YOU SAY

On the edge
of morning, in those moments
without a name, between darkness and dawn,
after the long night of making love and daring to dream,

we stand naked
at the window and look beyond
the bright incision of horizon, that opening
of blood and light where water meets sky and we see

the colors
beyond our sight, hints of infrared
and infinite, synaptic iridescence from water
to our weary flesh, yearning for wavelengths and light years,

so much
possibility pouring in makes us hard
and wanting each other but we cannot turn away
from the new light lifting and fresh, we stand soaking

our flesh
in the flood of sun and silence
and you say we should walk out on that flaming
path across the water to that place where time is still being born.

VALENTINE

For us, much of the harvest is in,
the day cools and the sun starts
its slow but sure farewell
with all its glow and mystery
and love is less about fire
than faithfulness, more
about silence than passion.

We have begun to admire silence
the way it opens its arms
and gathers us in and makes space.

I won't refuse your curious hands,
your stormy lips, but we both know
the climb is longer now,
and the momentary summit
is not our destination.

So take the hand that knows
your hand by heart.

MAKING LOVE

It happens mostly in silence, in bed,
the lights still on, propped on pillows,
you with your book, me with mine,
reading our individual lives to each other,
sometimes touching hands in the transitions
between chapters and sharing a piece of wisdom,
an interesting fact, a story that makes us laugh.
We are so close in our separateness
under the soft yellow silence falling on the pages
of our love, one night after another, like a story
that could go on, that you want to read
all the way through.

And sometimes when you are in the best part
of your book, I slide my hand up the tender slope
of your thigh and listen for the music of your passion
and you almost always put down the book.
The silence deepens. We give up on words,
on their small boxes of meaning. We give ourselves
to the silence, what we know can't
be contained in anything less spacious. And only
then do I hear the Ferris wheel of planets
turning with the rhythm of your steady heart,
the small beautiful songs that your muscles
make when you arch your back. I hear the way
dawn breaks in you, the wild light pouring
over the horizon. Only in the silence, we notice the holy
molecules of air settle softly on our one flesh.

IN THE DARKNESS

After it's come back
again after the years
of cautious hope
the shadow grows darker
and it's hard not to think about it.

Even in the middle of joy
all of a sudden the small
sound of cancer like an echo
bounces off the inside
of your skull and down
the arched canyon
of your ribs reverberating
in the darkness.

The forbidden word
we never say but always
know when we kiss
each other goodnight.

CHEMO

They measure you now with isotopes and enzymes,
weight, pulse, pressure,
the tingle in the toes.

They calculate their poisons carefully, they want
to kill you
but not too much, to douse the flames
and still keep the fire burning.

How do they measure the loss of desire,
how the yellow song
of the lily with its tongue of fire
fades to silence?

What is the cure for this desolate longing,
the feel of skin on skin,
insatiable hunger of your mouth,
for the river that would launch
our bodies by gravity and grace down the wild
rapids of our clear imperfect love?

HAWK RIDGE

On Hawk Ridge I watch the ancient
pilgrimage. They follow the high
road of water shimmer and wind race,
each feather gorged with air
and their wings cupping the blue
silence like sleek swimmers.
Some come gliding in, banking
on currents, hanging on thermals,
knowing the sweet surrender
of the whole body given and taken.
Others fall like hungry stones
out of the sky, eyes trained,
talons ready to clutch and tear.

I come here to dream of air
and the long canyons of luminescence,
to unshackle my body from the earth,
hacksaw the chains with long
cuts of October wind and then glide
on a zephyr of lapidary light.

Teach me to trust migration,
moon pull on the marrow in my bones.

DREAM

At last, sleeping in the garden
under the green sweet stars
of summer, I dream that death

does not matter. I see
the small stone cottage perched
on the cliff above the sea

like an old wise bird ready
for flight. It calls me to come
home to myself. All around

the house the lilies bloom and send
their honey syllables into the bright
air, heavy with salt. I breathe

in the blue waves that curl and crash.
The sun has begun its slow dance
of farewell, red round exclamation,

flash and dazzle on the darkening sea.
There is the sorrow of leaving,
the rapacious pull of earth, sea, light.

But their hands cannot hold me
and my fingers slip from their grasp.
At last, I step through the open door.

ROADSIDE MARKET

At the roadside market the colors
of tomato, eggplant, cucumber, sweet
corn dazzle in the high noon sun.

The farmer bags a dozen ears
for me and says it's a bumper year
for sunflowers, gestures toward
the field of bowing heads,
embodied exultation. The taut
green muscle of their stance, thick
leathery leaves, and then these faces,
fringed in essential luminescence,
following each day the arc of life,
always turning, submission of the finest
grace. Let the body work. It knows
the way to ecstasy and grief.

FACES

Three days in the Wind River Range
and I begin to know the face, the north
slope of Roaring Fork Mountain, its laugh

lines and hollows where the ice softens
and slides in July heat, crevice and cleft,
crack and fissure, time's long story

in the proud tall flesh of granite.
It stands here forgiving everything,
glinting with dawn, purpling with dusk,

its face battered by wind and sand,
its feet cut away by the wild constant river.
Year by year, it is scoured and reduced

finally to boulders, gravel, dust.

This is the plot of the whole story. Giving
and taking. Even the fire in the sun trades
light years with the stars; but all the laws

of physics don't make it easy. The way
the body of my lover thins, turns to ghost,
loses its fight and passion. The muscles

go slack, he's unsteady now, sometimes falls.
Goes from bed to couch, sits in the sun, speaks
softly, so softly. Tell me about mountains and mercy.

How many faces to memorize before you leave.

DREAM TWO

I stand by the open door of the white
shining house, all the houses on the island
are shades of sea foam and alabaster,
all lit by the full sun under a cloudless
ringing blue. I let my arms rise with a gust
of warm breeze. The white lilies bow,
their ecstatic faces sway and lift, their yellow
throats drink the light and sing.
When I am standing there in some kind
of prayer or salutation, I see you running

toward me, the beach sand flying from your feet,
your hair ruffled by the wind, your eyes laughing.
And just when you are in arm's reach, when I
am about to pull your body to my body, I feel
something lash across my face, some invisible
filament of fear or recognition. And I am
standing there next to the open door alone,
with my arms empty except for the rippling air
and the soft wind full of salt from the infinite sea.

PRAYER AT DAWN

I come here to greet the dawn, say a prayer
of hope to stretch my life toward the light.
I come to the center point of the spinning
world, this place of intersection where
the bright music of a little stream empties
into the waiting lake, where white gulls dance
their feathered alleluias down wide aisles
of jubilant dawn, where golden-eyed ducks
disappear beneath the shimmering surface
and emerge newly baptized and gleaming,
where the willow's spring branches of spun
honey are filled with a choir of blackbirds,
their voices catch fire as they rise as one
congregation into the sky, flashing ebony wings.

I bow and join my voice to the music of wind
and water, sprinkle cornmeal and turquoise into
the current and remember Minnie and Cornelius,
Nellie and John, Margaret and Cornelius and all
the ancestors whose names I have forgotten
and whose names I have never known. I listen
as all the relations gather, driven here by the wind,
pooling around my ankles in the cold water.
In every tongue the voices enter, my veins swell
with names, eternal faces and everlasting hands.

LAKE SUPERIOR

Days on end this lake is a gray
lady of grief, lifeless and brooding,
sighing a litany of lamentations.

And other days she's sparkling, sequined
every color, shining silver and jewels,
a soaring descant of desire.

Perhaps she mimics us, no more or less
than a mirror for our most extravagant
longings and our unfaithful despair.

But not our mirror alone, come the dawn,
she takes the light and oh the dance she does,
she lifts the light and shakes it,

her whole body shivers and delights,
every fluid syllable filled with luminescence,
every cell a refraction of praise.

AFTER SAILING

After sailing all day
through the diamonds
and silk of Superior,
the rhythm of the waves
still in my body, I dream
the wind sings in my bones,
hollow flutes for a symphony
of luster and I am

nothing

solid, stationary, past,
but permeable and empty
of everything but breath
pulled in and out by the moon.
The soul of the world shines
everywhere and even the green
hills on the shore are wave
after wave of sibilant light.

I am easily confused
about things of importance now.
I count my deepest obligations
to gardens, trails, silence.
I follow the wind's paws
on the blue water to catch
a final puff of breeze before turning
the bow toward the harbor. I am

nothing

but skin and bits of grape,
the dregs of intoxication.

GEESE IN MOONLIGHT

We fly in the rain tonight
drops
of moonlight
impatient
to be done
with the long journey

take our turn at the point

and when the weakness
comes
as it always does
we are lifted
by the strength of the young
swimmers in the front rows
who open the way with their proud
bodies

feel the pull in the hollow
of our bones
cup the edges
of feathers to find the last ounce
of speed give ourselves to the sure
currents of air take the bite
of the cold rain and hope
for sun
come morning.

With every wing beat
we call
we must
this one note
that echoes
down the fierce flute
of our necks the one song
long pour of longing
for home.

ABOVE THE LAKE

White wisps of eagle wings and swallow
tails fly in the cool blue above the lake,
the wide, wise pinions of owls hover,
ghosts of gulls glide, all that is air, light,
feather and filigree, plume and pirouette
through the broad, reaching summer sky.

In these high clouds Jesus speaks of birds
that neither sow nor reap, how every day
we should pour our grief like water
on the thirsty ground and take to flight.
Shake the shackles from our legs, tilt
our faces to the sky-writing clouds and read.

Bones of earth but the air inside whistles
and soars. Flesh feeds on muscle,
wheat, worry; wide eyes will not stop
searching the cloud-scudded sky. Why try to hang
on to anything but wonder, anything but wonder.

GARDEN

Take the dead bodies of the leaves with their particular
faces, generous hands, all the green memories

that still sing in their crumbling veins and fold them
into the soil with reverence and laughter.

Follow closely the ritual of the seeds. Choose only
the promises, hold them in your cupped hand,

feel the weight of all their mercy. Breathe on the hard
husks to soften them and give them courage.

Tell them: Listen to the green songs in the dark earth,
let the river enter, trust your longing for light.

Space them in God's footsteps. Sift the finest soil over
the small organs of hope with reverence and laughter.

Make your covenant before the first rain falls. Will your
hands be open? Will your mouth hunger for the fertile

taste of earth in the fruit, the sweetness of patient days
mellowing the flesh. Will you trust the whole story,

will you be faithful? And when the time comes, will
you give yourself with reverence and laughter?

LITANY ON THE BEACH

Early morning on the warm beach,
a momentary Rosetta stone of glyphs
and runes, tracings of birds, mollusks,

and the moon's work, waits now
for the sea's erasure. The fisherman
is here again as sure as the sun's climb

out of the morning mist, already
dancing with his net and hungry eyes,
looking for lightning in the aqua water,

his fine mesh of dreams draped
over his arms and shoulders,
then flung out in a perfect circle.

In a fluid glissando his feet turn
in the white sand, his muscled arms
arc through the spume thrown up

by the surrendering waves.
Then he gathers it in, closes the circle,
pulls the net slowly to himself.

He seems to smile at the small fish
taken from this immensity of ocean,
then goes on dancing down the wide

aisles of the waking light, every
morning a litany of faith and longing.
Step now to the ocean's edge,

say your prayers into glinting luster,
throw your net, fling yourself
open toward the horizon.

IMAGES IN SLEEP

Is this house with its red door
        some part of your journey
                you haven't opened but calls

to you in words you are just
        beginning to hear like a song
                in the wind? Are your arms

strong enough to listen?
        Are all your belongings
                willing to be given away?

Do not turn your back
        on this voice that beckons,
                carry it like a promise

through the gate of dawn.
        Let it come to you like some distant
                friend whose bond was never broken.

Take up the conversation
        as if only yesterday you sat
                musing under the purple lilacs

talking of the way forward, the fire
        that embers in your bones, the longing
                that tugs persistently on your sleeve.

You could rush off into everything
        you already know the answer or
                you could sit here in the shadow

of the question, of what might be
        possible, if you picked the apple
                from the tree in the middle of the garden.

HIKING AUTUMN

All day I've been shuffling
through the colors of autumn,
the hiking trail like an aisle
of light through a crowd of high couture
dressed in stunning silks and satins,
yellow fire of finch wings,
blaze of ruby, goldfish fin
lacquered and layered,
every leaf slick with dew,
the extravagant spectacle of shine.

The path is littered
with triumph, death, devotion,
the clatter of decay;
my footsteps press the fallen faces
into the earth as it cools
patient and unquestioning.

Death would be a lot easier
if we didn't have to give up so much,
all the windows of the body,
all the rituals of longing.

The path comes out of the woods
and circles this lazy pasture,
three black velvet horses
with their soft muzzles
pluck the last sweet grasses.
Curious about my footsteps,
they lift their heads in unison
like three elegant machines
made of steel and ecstasy,
they call to me
across the wire fences.

BETWEEN US

Sometimes the distance
        between us is light years,
                you in your dying, me

in my planning to keep
        the flowers watered and
                get the house painted

before the frost comes
        early in the fall. Death seeps
                into every syllable and finally

nothing is free of finitude,
        the counting of days,
                the names of the guardian angels.

But today you ask me to massage
        your feet and hands, so I sit
                on the edge of your hospital bed

and try to feel the marrow in your brittle
        bones, to soften the tendons taut as anchor
                lines in a harsh wind, to taste the ripe fruit

of now, to inhabit together the deepening
        silent sorrow. We have already entered
                the empty house of grief, you saying goodbye

to everything that touches your skin,
        me facing your banishment from
                this world, from your side of the bed.

WITHOUT KNOWING

Tell me what you are thinking
    about living and dying
        how the flesh is branded

by the fire of touch, how the hand
    learns to open and close around
        its memories, tell me what

you have forgotten and how it returns when
    you're not looking, tell me about the silence,
        syllables frozen by the cold creeping up your spine,

use your hand like a map and trace
    the ways that are still uncharted,
        directions that will only be given

in the going, in the figuring it out
    as we stumble into these starless nights
        of unknowing, groping for anything solid.

How will you make this final passage
    through the narrow canyon, how many
        pints of blood will you sacrifice to the gods?

Let me listen to the crumbling
    in your bones, let me kiss you
        where the pieces have fallen out.

I know I am only a guest in this land
    of dying, I am a stranger to this language
        of leaving, but I will walk next to you.

I will hold your hand in the dark, I will
    listen to the silence between your words.
        Yes, I am going to the same far country.

I will follow the same impossible passage
    through the furnace that now strips you
        of everything, that tears at your flesh

until you are only a whisper, a slightness,
    a quiet that settles deeper and slower
        and yet some wild essence of yourself

that bold and confident man who stepped
    across my threshold carrying an armful
        of flowers with that holy longing on your lips.

MAKING A BOWL WITH MY HANDS

First, I collect bowls from potters,
their hands caked with clay,
their wheels whirring at art fairs
and in small shops on gravel roads;
I develop a benign obsession feeling
the weight of bowls in my hands,
texture of glazed and unglazed,
patterns of leaves, drips, lyrical lines,
deep, shallow, ridged, round, fluted;
hues and shades of emerald, copper,
crimson, dusk, dawn, shadow, shine.

Then, one day, after he's had another
slow drip of chemotherapy and another
scan of bones and brain, I take a bowl
from the cupboard and have cereal for supper
alone at the kitchen counter because again
he is too tired to eat. The blue cosmic
edge of the bowl swirls into galaxies, litanies
of lamentations among the planets and stars,
all the constellations of dream and desire.
So, finally, I cup my hands together
to make a bowl, each finger curved inward
to hold everything and then I open them
slowly, as if to let everything flow out, as if
I could hold anything in my small hands.

BY BREATH

If you hold the hand of a dying man
it will change you. You will learn to count
each breath, sit in silence in your own soft skin

and let time take as long as it wants.
You will learn the sun's ritual, the round path
it walks each day, the discipline and the bright wonder.

The tick of the clock will not annoy you
and if there is a word or two, you will listen as if
your life depended on it. Not much else will matter,

the dishes, the laundry, the paint
peeling in the summer heat. Sitting at the side
of his bed even when he is sleeping will be enough.

You may not be able to say exactly what
has changed but you will pronounce your name
as if it were hyphenated, wedded to river, orbit, earth.

You will watch trees bow down before the wind.
You will breathe one breath at a time as if your
life depended on it, your whole life depended on it.

ETIOLOGY

I

We are fallen angels not able to resist
the body and touch the real presence
in its sanctuary not able to live by word alone
but bread and the heat of the flesh

how the eyes compose a symphony
how the sweet sweat rises on the small
of the back mist at dawn
how the chest fills with light

we have forfeited our wings for this
to trace the curve of a thigh with our tongue
to follow like an explorer a dark vein of gift
that rivers through the land of ecstasy

how touch can lift us into flight all life's cargo
worry sacrifice devotion made weightless

II

Near the end now you say almost no words the body
is our language a perfect slice of ripe peach
placed in your mouth the juice glistens on your ghost lips
each part of the body tenderly washed

with the womb warm water tuck you into bed
pull the covers up under your chin
massage the long legs that now are mostly bone
kiss the little tufts of white hair that the radiation

didn't touch if we are not angels
how would we know these secret rituals of mercy

CASTING OFF

You will not give up your body
reduced to sticks and a pulse
still you want to stay
in the house
of light
where the daisies
lift their plain and beautiful faces
and the poppies parade
their regal silks in the garden
outside your vigil window
the yellow lilies
all you grew to love.

The cargo is unloaded
day by day almost invisible
the thick lines
are cast off
the heavy chain of reason
hauled up
with its anchor
of logic.

Still you want to walk
through the house
over and over
one small labored step
after another
looking at your legs
willing them to move
retracing your steps
in all the streets
it was your pleasure to walk.

At last
a small round moan
rises from your marrow
and the dark entanglements of disease
a small round moan

with each breath
strains against the tide
that pulls you
at last
the silent sea.

VISITATION

In the last month
sometimes he saw things heard things
a cat on the mantel or on the window sill
do you see the cat
he asked his eyes staring off
into the distance between himself
and what was approaching
do you hear the cat meow he asked

For a dog person who directed
that the ashes of his favorite Alex
be buried with him
these were unusual sightings unusual sounds
I thought the cancer's cellular explosions
in the brain or perhaps the physical
memories of the quaint guest house
in Guanajuato in chilly January
when the cat came pawing at our
warm door and he let it in to sit purring
on his lap in front of the little fireplace

On the day he died
in those first hours of drowning
after everyone had left
and the hospital bed was the only
presence in the living room
and the sheets still held the shape
of his body
a black and white cat
showed up on the front steps
looking in through the screen door
the dogs barked frantically
until it turned and walked
quietly away

APPEARANCES

finding you in pieces
and places I can't expect
surprised by tablespoons
of tomato paste
you put in the freezer

books you've left a place marked
a clipping of Salisbury cathedral
stashed in the world atlas for our next trip

walking the Split Rock trail
your footsteps still echo

packing your shirts to give away
I repeat our ritual
button your collar
kiss your fresh shaved face

bowing to the yellow buds
in the rose garden
fragrance of all our anniversaries
your smile
in the folded silk of their petals

appearing in cantaloupes
smell of lemons
taste of caramel apples
anchovies capers lamb chops

paying for Prosecco
at the liquor store
the man wonders at the tears
but doesn't ask
walking day after day
sad gratitude
like pebbles
in my shoes
unpredicted visits
your only touch

DID YOU KNOW

when you told me
your name
and took my hand walking in the park
how many knots were you untying
how many stones were you rolling away
did you let the current take you
did you worry about betrayal

did you know then
that the day would come too soon
the sadness that no flower
could name
the distance that no hand could
reach across

when you let the wind
play in your hair like that
was it so I would fall in love
so I would never
leave you
would be your last kiss
your last goodbye

did you know then
how the river would carry us
how the light would fall
on the pink peonies in the garden
how we would drink wine on the deck
and watch their satin gowns
tremor in the breeze

when you looked at me like that
across the room
were you already planning
to kiss me in St. Peter's square
in front of Jesus in the manger
and all the hovering angels

were you counting the days then
did you feel
the poison in your blood
did you know you would
die in summer
steal all the colors
from the garden
all the vowels from the stars

until slowly I could learn
to say
your name again
softly softly
your name

MEMORY

It would be enough for God
to be memory
precise attention to every instant
everlastingly to hold each one
like a drop on the tongue
of honey or blood
the word's immeasurable weight
the nod
the touch
in the moment
never forgotten.

On your birthday
I can't remember the last gift
or if we ate at home what I cooked
to make your day happy
but when I'm not trying
scenes come in avalanches
at the sound of your wind chimes
the scent of garlic
a yellow rosebud edged in red
and there we are
sitting beside a stream
in northern Italy
as if it was our own language
two prosciutto sandwiches
and a bottle of red wine
the name of the town
the river unknown
the date I can only come close.

But what I know
is that your hands
are large and soft
as you pour the wine
and there is a point in the conversation
when you lift your face
to the sun

and stay like that for a breath
a sigh
and the river pours
over the round rocks
and the sun settles
on your face.

THE CHILL

I haven't been warm
since they took you
in the black body bag
out the front door
the whole house is empty
hollow sounds the incessant clock.

I put on all the lights
play the music loud
heap more wood on the dying fire
wonder if my skin
will ever shed this gelid shiver.

Yesterday on my hike
the ravaged nest on the path
months old but still the gall
and guts what once were wings.

Three nights in a row
the hard frost serious ice
on the puddles not the scrim
that will melt by noon.

My winter coat already in October
hands gone numb
digging the last carrots and beets
from the withered garden.

But here in the corner tiny white flowers
bloom in the bitter wind
star faces in the gray afternoon
shine still in the bone deep chill.

It might be enough
if God is possibility.

TRAJECTORY

How does one common seed do all this in a short season,
singularity in the garden, big bang in the ordinary soil?

A rough leather stalk six feet high, heft of thigh,
muscled reach without doubt or divergence, straight

as the beatitude, pure of heart, and the calloused hands
veined and viscid, work their alchemy of phototropic lust.

All this ardor and devotion to lift a face fringed
in yellow finch wings, fire flung out in essence of dazzle,

gold ruffle of passion, mane of tempest and heat.
Centered on the steadfast stalk a thousand eyes trace

the arc of the sun as daily adoration and desire, fractals
of absolute attention, sublime stare before the noble bow.

Fruitfulness turns to gift, the heavy head does not lift
or track the shortening days, the fierce engine slumps

in the cold and the seeds soften, loosen their hold,
drop and scatter, give themselves to the moist soil.

SOLSTICE

How to trust the orbit of light
in the long ellipse
of loneliness
bone chill
dark by four in the afternoon
when grief clambers up and down
the cold corridor of spine.
How to trust the odyssey of the heart
yearning in its endless journey
for home
the chair on the sunny porch
purple lilacs on the breeze
a hand to hold.
How to trust the return
when every surface is glazed
in glass untouchable.
How to trust
the sleeping tubers
of the peony and iris
to fling their sumptuous silks
about the green garden ever again.
How to believe
in the cosmic circuits
that swing from chaos
to apocalypse among the old planets
and the newborn fires.
How to trust the affections
of light
warming the cedars
so the small avalanche of snow
slips from the emerald branch
and the fierce river in the heart
begins to flow.

III.

LAZARUS UNBOUND

It was a small wish
only slightly exotic
for northern Minnesota
Acer Palmatum
Japanese Maple
feathered crimson lava shine
so I planted it in early September
as the arborist directed
with precise specifications
six inches of black dirt
and compost in the deep hole
the root ball unwrapped
and the roots loosened a bit
so they would stretch
explore extend
and after the last leaf fell
that first autumn
I wrapped it in burlap
against the deep chill
gave it all the attention it needed
so that in spring
the buds were bulging
every branch
beaded in promissory jewels
until the late frost
no one expected
erasure
black beaks shriveled unsung
in the lengthening days
in the bright sun
not a single one spared
bare branches through the summer green
still I left it in the ground
for another circle of seasons
an isotope of Lazarus running
in my blood
and spring has come round again
and the fiddles of the ferns

are unfolding
and still those maple branches
are bare as grief
but now I ply the shovel
my instep memorizing again
the rhythm of all things.

SOARING

the windless trees shake
with squirrels
acrobats amnesiacs
they have to be to launch
their bodies hurtling across space
to another branch that dips
and springs
so much forgetfulness of gravity
and failure

the spiral chase up a trunk
and then their long jumps
from tree to tree
sometimes taking a tender limb
almost to breaking
scrambling up again
and soaring

will you leap
allow yourself to be framed by sky
fling yourself into flight
the trapeze artist says this is the easy part
even a somersault or two
anyone can master
and the hard part
allowing yourself to be caught
not grasping not bending toward
the catcher must do all the work
and you must let it happen
in the cool empty air above the crowd
surrender

FINDING HIM

If the hammock is hanging
in its slothful slouch
and the grass is nearly
to your knees,
how much time do you have?
If the circus is coming
to town on the day
you should be writing
your will and you are accepted
into the sideshow,
what will they name your act?
Will you tie yourself in knots
or just hang on to the largest
Lipezzaner stallion
galloping around the galaxy
at warp speed?

NESTING

With all the green threads of hope
in the fine weave of your body,
make me a nest in the branches
of your arms. Make it warm
against the storm. Gather the tender
grasses softened by the weight
of sorrow and snow, the abandoned
kite string woven in the fingers of oak,
pieces of purple yarn from the mitten
still clenched tight in the fist of ice,
and dreams, plenty of spring dreams.
Stitch it all together with your closest
attention, interlace the laughter
and the pain, braid the strands
of gladness, grief, longing.
Line the safe circle with the softest
down stolen from the warmth
close to your heart. Then, call me
with your song. Do that dance
with your fancy feathers. Lure me home.

SPRING LIGHT

The kind morning light precisely
through the spring window
fills the small of his back
with a pool of honey
and the whole Eden garden comes
alive in lemon luster
even the stoic pines
with every candle on fire.

All things are greedy
for light
charmed into some new version
of themselves
circle upon circle
of season and promise
lift sing from seed or root
the urge that needs
only this amber touch.

Even where the shadows are deep
in the dappled saffron and shade
the ferns are rising
their hopes still spiraled tight
in the green surge of their bodies.

GIVEN NAME

Three eagles in the sky
name him
a name pulled
from the long book of names
published by the planet.

Eagle wings
brush his body,
his eyes echo cloudless blue
and the vast thrumming light
enters his bones.

Three eagles in the sky
lift and circle
in their naming rite,
his bones are hollowed
by their dance, empty of everything

but wind and the scent it carries,
his mouth closes
upon all its imperfect words
and their secret
slavery.

Three eagles trace
a circle of silence inside him
everywhere the center
nowhere the reaching circumference,
the wings take him.

He kisses his love
in that music of wings
in that pure light under the circling
eagles
in the soft blue silence.

OVER THE THRESHOLD

Frankie in her final breaths
black cold nose
pressed against my palm
soft coat of black and brown curls
the whole tender mystery of her
brings back all the grief
of losses small and insurmountable.
I am learning to sense
the presence
of the dead
how close they are
how they go back and forth
over the threshold
how they are still curious
about the mystery of days
how they miss the body.
I am learning
loss is the cost
of love
and suffering is common
as grass
and to hold it all in the nest
of the heart as if each moment
is another promise in its fragile shell
colored and shaped
absolutely particular dog or person.

PROVINCETOWN BEACH

Walk with me down this soft sand
crescent to the lighthouse
where the red roses tango

in the sea breeze, twist and sway
in their shocking silks, their yellow
throats singing lucent arias

in the hot afternoon of summer.
Always near the lighthouses
mounds and scatterings of crimson.

You might think the keepers
of the lights were romantic,
seeding roses during their long

days of loneliness, waiting to light
the flashing lamp for another night,
but the roses came from wrecks

on shoals, splintered dreams and lives lost.
Treasures washed ashore along with rose
hips, dysentery's cure on the long voyages.

So let us lay our bodies down here
next to the roses that still remember,
settle into the forgiving sand, let the sun

lap over our coppered bodies, breeze
blow in the flutes of our bones, salt
spray soften our small losses into song.

BLACKBIRDS

A frenzy of blackbirds rises into the washed blue
and wrinkles the sky with their wings, wheel of fire
divides and merges, Ezekiel's chrysolite and electrum,
settles in the swamp, every bare stalk and bronzed
cattail decorated with an ebony alleluia.

No straight lines but a wild waltz
in drifts and gyrations, they dive and ascend
from marsh to swale, arc over the lush hills,
torches and lightning, black oiled wings
shine as they chatter, turn the seasons

in spiral and song, seek the wetlands, the mist,
pry seeds from the ripe fruit. And in all things
the pulse, pouring out of the sky or seeping up
from the wet soil, in all things the sound of wings,
in all things the roaring of the soaring wings.

REFLECTION

In between whispered syllables
of fire and affection
in the spaces between
stacked vertebrae
I count and kiss
between the litany of ribs
there is a reflecting pool of silence
where tenderness
echoes
a second gift
of seeing the first gift given and received
an awareness
in the moment after the moment
has passed
a third thing
not you not me
but both of us held
in that silence
that ripens like peaches
blush and juice
the skin of time opened
flesh that burns and comforts
only in our mirrored glance
do we see the breath's cargo
cosmic dust ancient argon
connecting every genesis
in the body's vow.

CONSTELLATION

If you are walking hand in hand
under the moonlight
counting the fierce
and holy stars as they appear

and you forget the name of a constellation
you can make up your own story
about the warrior
who falls in love with the foreign prince

how they each give up their kingdoms
for another land
how the stars outline the shield
of his strength and the outstretched

hand of the other's question
how the darkness is pushed back
how their story catches in the web of light
and names their own piece of sky.

TO SAY A WORD

We walk the granite ridge
spine of earth's primordial body
the ancient columns and arches
protecting the leaping neurons
of ages epics evolutions
where the white pines shush
every thought and footstep
to take the long view over the valley
where acres of sunlight fall
upon the umber fields
and the inlaid diamonds
set among emerald evergreens
and where the sky hovers
vast and vanishing.
There we dare to say a word
almost silence
syllable of promise
so simple so effortless
as if the cancers of the night
could be tamed
and the unhinged galaxies
could learn a new story.

THE HUMAN BEING

After working five days
at the forge of time
turning out sky fires
essences of air and earth
pouring the waters down the troughs of heaven
shaping delicate seeds
and the long
story of each one
silence to blossom
tendril to gift
cone calyx stamen scent
machinery of molecule and cell
chemical vocabulary
synapse axon blood
circus of animals
fin feather scale
buzz bark song
finally finally
the human being
awe in the bone
longing that won't quit
in the gut
instruments of ecstasy
lips where the word
shapes dreams
heart where this idea rises
slow dancing
barefoot on the cool summer grass
bodies moving in moonlight.

UPON WAKING

Last night the honey bees
deposited their sweet nectar
in the small spaces of my spine
their sticky feet tickling the tendons
tensioned with knowledge and failure
their small songs echoing
into the cortical chambers prying
into the hippocampus with prisms
of light seeping into the networks
of neurons. All the work of bees
and childhood memories
songs of jonquils and daffodils
all the shades of buds and shoots
sage sap plum and sea
synapsing in the cellular entanglements
in the soft ethers of dreams.
Waking into the spring light
your body warm against my body
flooded with amber and mercy
the color and taste of honey.

DANCING AT THE WEDDING

A dance floor is not a boxing ring,
not a stage for political speeches
on marriage equality or dramatic
soliloquies on all the subtle messages
meant to keep the status quo going just so,
although the lights are bright.
It is not an open field under the merciful stars.
At the Knights of Columbus Hall
the pictures of the bishop and the pope
look on with earnest judgment.
Still, we danced and held each other,
joined by friends and family familiar and new,
we claimed a circle of light for two men
to dance and twist, strut and sing,
to be the father of the groom and his partner
at the wedding, strands in the fabric
of family woven by the spinning stars.

THRESHOLDS

Every face every word
a doorway
every doubt a threshold
how the beach
is neither water nor land

space in between where every step
forward or retreat
makes a mark in the sand
not for long

if every time we look
at the stars
we hear them beckoning
scan the horizon
and notice its invitation

the world keeps calling
in sun and shadow
moon breathing over the lake

have you placed the soles of your feet
against the dewy grass

have you noticed how the smallest
bone in your body
vibrates with bird song
wind song and the shush of the grass

and what can be said
about the threshold of the lips

NOTES

"Eyes Wide Open Exhibit" reflects on the American Friends Service Committee's exhibition on the wars in Iraq and Afghanistan which features a pair of boots honoring each U.S. military casualty and a circle of common shoes honoring the civilians who have died. The exhibit started in January 2004 when the US casualties in Iraq numbered 500. In May 2007, when the casualties in Iraq numbered 3,500, the exhibit was split into smaller state-based exhibits.

"Ask The Children" is based on "Trauma Exposure and Psychological Reactions to Genocide Among Rwandan Children" by Atle Gyregrov, Leila Gupta, Rolf Gjestad and Eugenie Mukanoheli in *Journal of Traumatic Stress,* Vol. 13, No. 1 (2000).

"Heaven" begins with two lines from "Homo Will Not Inherit" by Mark Doty in *Atlantis*, HarperCollins, 1995.

"Out of Nothing" contains the quotation "continual fluctuations in the nothingness are generating and subsuming innumerable universes" from an interview with a professor of physics, specialist in string theory, which appeared in the TIAA-CREF newsletter sometime in 2009.

ABOUT THE AUTHOR

Gary J. Boelhower, PhD is professor of theology and religious studies at The College of St. Scholastica in Duluth, Minnesota, where he teaches courses in healthcare ethics; living, dying and grieving; spirituality and resilience; contemporary moral issues and leadership. He has held several leadership positions in higher education including Dean of Graduate Studies and Vice President for Academic Affairs. He is the co-founder of the Center for Spirituality and Leadership at Marian University in Fond du Lac, Wisconsin. He has consulted with a broad range of organizations on values integration, conflict resolution, team spirit, mission and strategy, ethical issues in health and human services, and the respectful workplace. He has facilitated executive development programs and provides conference presentations on dialogue, wise decision-making, authentic leadership, values and vision, appreciative inquiry, and professional development. He has published a dozen education texts as well as many scholarly articles on servant leadership, practical wisdom, quality processes, values integration, educational assessment, religious pluralism and process theology. His poems have been published in the following anthologies: *Beloved on the Earth: 150 Poems of Grief and Gratitude* by Holy Cow! Press, *Trail Guide to the Northland Experience in Prints and Poetry* by Calyx Press Duluth, *Response: Poetry and Prints from the Lake Superior Writers and the Northern Printmakers Alliance* by Calyx Press Duluth, and *County Lines: 87 Minnesota Counties 130 Minnesota Poets* by Loonfeather Press, as well as in the journals *Freshwater Review, Out of Words,* and *Willow Review.*

CPSIA information can be obtained at www.ICGtesting.com
Printed in the USA
BVOW07s0638290813

329811BV00002B/56/P